COLLECTING
silence

COLLECTING
silence

ULRIKE NARWANI

RONSDALE

RONSDALE PRESS
3350 West 21st Avenue
Vancouver, B.C., Canada V6S 1G7
www.ronsdalepress.com

Typesetting: Julie Cochrane, in New Baskerville 11 pt on 13.5
Cover Design: Julie Cochrane
Paper: 70 lb. Envirographic 100—FSC certified with 100% post-consumer
    waste, totally chlorine-free and acid-free

Ronsdale Press wishes to thank the following for their support of its publishing
program: the Canada Council for the Arts, the Government of Canada through
the Canada Book Fund, the British Columbia Arts Council, and the Province
of British Columbia through the Book Publishing Tax Credit Program.

Canada Council   Conseil des arts
for the Arts   du Canada

Canada

BRITISH COLUMBIA
ARTS COUNCIL
An agency of the Province of British Columbia

Library and Archives Canada Cataloguing in Publication

Narwani, Ulrike, author
    Collecting silence / Ulrike Narwani.

Issued in print and electronic formats.
ISBN 978-1-55380-487-1 (print)
ISBN 978-1-55380-488-8 (ebook) / ISBN 978-1-55380-489-5 (PDF)

    I. Title.

PS8627.A772C65 2017   C811'.6   C2016-907438-2   C2016-907439-0

At Ronsdale Press we are committed to protecting the environment. To this
end we are working with Canopy and printers to phase out our use of paper
produced from ancient forests. This book is one step towards that goal.

Printed in Canada by Island Blue, Victoria, B.C.

for Dru, Tara, Anita and Julian,
all my love

ACKNOWLEDGEMENTS

Many thanks to Yvonne Blomer, inspiring guide and mentor, for her invaluable insights that helped put the spit and polish on this manuscript. Thanks to Patrick Lane, Terry Ann Carter, Garth Martens, Barbara Pelman, Wendy Morton, for opening possibilities, and Russell Thorburn, for sensing the underlying trajectory of my work. Thanks to my poet friends for their attentive eye: Judith Castle, Zoe Dickinson, Susan Braley, Gisela Ruebsaat, Sidney Bending, Marlene Grand-Maître, Daniel Scott, Dvora Levin, Sheila Martindale. Deep appreciation to my parents, Karin and Gerhard Conradi, for a home full of books and music, access to art, theatre, dance, travel—the wider world. Thanks to my daughters: Tara for finding nuggets in beginner's dross, and Anita for insisting I follow my own path. My gratitude to Ronald Hatch of Ronsdale Press for taking a leap and publishing *Collecting Silence*.

A number of poems or their earlier versions have previously been published:

"Blue and White Pottery," first prize in *FreeFall*.

"Dun," honourable mention in *Vallum*.

"After the Opera on Humboldt Street," first prize in *Island Writer*.

"Never Too Late," in *Contemporary Verse 2*.

"An Offering," in *Poems from Planet Earth*.

"Hollows" and "The Fourth Monk," in chapbooks ed. by Patrick Lane.

"seaweed/rocking on slow waves/a passing ferry" and "an eagle/ circling the sun . . . /field of daisies," in *Haiku Canada Members' Anthology*.

I am thinking of last leaves.

The beauty of beginning.

—PATRICK LANE

CONTENTS

~ I ~

– I –

transplanting seedlings

a tree frog

on her hand

Prayer Flags

We walk to a temple above Gangtok.
Prayer flags span the road between stands of dark pine.
White with age, they stream in the wind,
wishes tied to a string.

A glass-enclosed room. Hundreds of oil lamps burn,
a bed for the dead, their long goodbye.
Rosy-cheeked monks polish them one by one.
Nearby, a room for meditation,
benches, cushions for kneeling,
drums, gongs, a place for quiet thought and song.
We slip inside, hug the wall,
listen, eyes closed, in the dusky light.
A monk rushes up, asks us to leave.

We stumble outside.
Hurry past prayer wheels.
Set them turning.
Hands skimming faith.
The letters foreign.

Though shut out
I know about incomprehensible words
circling night after night,
lamp fire added to lamp fire until the dark
grows ill with desire.

I know that between stands of dark pine
our deepest surrender
flutters with myriad others
on a continual thin line.

Never Too Late

It is never too late, he says, to give a hand.
The clock on the mantel barely moves a hand.

The spider's web is rimmed with winter frost.
The spider, lost, hides in the child's sleeping hand.

Pigeons scrabble for winter's paltry crumbs
scattered by an old man, his frozen red hand.

Honking cars, black slush, a man marooned at night.
He looks around, but cannot find a hand.

A pianist in a bar as the evening shuts down
lets loose with his rare-dream hand.

A young man ties his Countess Mara necktie.
The silk slips smoothly through his skilled hand.

Rapunzel lets down her hair, her pomegranate hair.
Her lover climbs to her, hand over hand.

The moon slides down the roof of my house.
I go outside to catch it, stretch out my white hand.

Jumping into Water

They say if you jump in often enough
water will grow wings.

A jump past your skin to the heart of things.

Do you remember the hiding spot under the big leaf
where you listened to the rain? A rain house.
A finger was enough to enter the world.
And the newborn mice in the furrow of a field?
Skin pink against brown clumps of soil,
heartbeat transparent.

But the world had different ambitions.
People sketched far-fetched horizons.
Chuckwagons headed westward,
gouged ruts.
Promises gilded gold.
The Alamo fell.

They say if you jump in often enough
a baobab house will rise
thickening with each rain,
a gourd filled with water for "the dry."

They say if you jump in often enough
you will not drown.

The Fish

You smile as if
you had caught that one fish, the only fish,
mouth, gills, tail
all there, tiny and moving and now
what to do
in your amazement, with it lying in your hand.

You were five and did not see that the strange moving
was dying.

You smile like then,
stepping into a new strangeness,
rocking in a rocking chair as you tell me about her,
the catch and hold,
only now you can read the signals,
understand the pumping-gill need,
the blue-fleshed fragility
as you dive in.

A Reminiscent Shape

The deer are missing.
They pass through my garden year-round
regular as the need to eat.
Foes—what did they not devour—then a kind of familial.
Eyes closing in.

Their absence. What to make of it? Until one day
I stumble upon a birth
dropped as if in passing on the stone pathway.

Only a reminiscent shape, a touch bigger
than a man's footprint.
Flattened face, recognizable still,
mouth open for first breath.

Smell, that round sprout,
its shroud.

A small brownness
something like down
flits with each snatch of wind,
and settles back.

Unlike the goslings
that just tested wings.

Sandy Path

There is a bird inside my eyes
even at night
even in rain, snow.

It sees you, my father
in youth
no longer young
sitting by a sun-warmed sandy path
long legs crossed
wearing shorts
hands behind your head
thinning hair still brown
the fragile beat of your heart
stopped once before
a dot, no
a red spider
racing across time's page.

You float on a river of music
all the instruments are boats
bearing gifts.

That was then.

Time stretches
like a child
towards a new toy.

You, sweet Arya, granddaughter
hands half the size of mine
explore my bathroom drawer.
Short brush, small box. Red treasure.
I stroke the red
apply it to your lips, two bows.
You apply red to my lips
a boat going over waves,
close the box, put box and brush back.
All is order.
Nothing has changed
only colour.

What winged in your eyes, dearest father
as you sat by that sandy path?
Did you see, far in the distance
a colour
changed?
A red spider tracing a line?

Netsuke

When was it
I stood in a swirl of monarch butterflies
and became tree?

Loon-song evening
warm ivory.

Joggers on a wet-sun hill
hooked by light.

Trees a toss of gold
air wide.

When was it, mother, we sat on a bench
above the sweep of river?

In loving memory on a bronze plaque
buffed by chamois wind.

High-rise night windows
mute faces lit within.

When was it
that blaze of orange
the Fabergé dawn?

Morning moon low in the sky
transparent.

I carved it all
stored it on the shelf of my mind.

When do I gift the wind?

Netsuke: Miniature sculptures used as belt fasteners in 17th-century Japan,
and now highly prized as exquisite art objects.

The Morning Is Too Straight

The morning is too straight
Clouds vanish before I can follow

There was a time my son sat on a beach with pail and shovels
Drew sharks in the sand next to flowers

I sift sand for incandescence
A stranded jellyfish, iridescence faded.

This Foreign Language

Food stalls in Chatuchak market, Bangkok. What looks like
slabs of blood. A boy eats wriggling shrimp on rice.

Hindu gods, carried out to sea, dissolve. Prayers, song, dance.
My video camera is stolen. There's a hole in my journey.

Home looks different from above clouds. Mountain peaks
hide like a family of quail in tall grass. Is home far?

I discover edible wild berries: Oregon grape, kinnikinnick,
salal. Strange words. They knock on the roof of my mouth.

Patches of snow on the fields; or is it salt?
This foreign language. Birds are not bothered.

Buoy

At the water's edge
is an empty canoe
open to the pouring
in of starlight

—Eleonore Schönmaier,
  "Weightless"

Sky heavy
with cloud.
Cormorants huddle
on a buoy, wings closed.
Grey sea laps and laps.
Thoughts of my daughter slip off the ledge
uprooted. We do not speak.
The tide rakes
seaweed strips, torn pledge
at the water's edge

where oysters clamp shut
at the slightest touch,
no eye left outside.
Tongues of mist troll
crevice and nook
our severed ties. I miss you.
Awash in detritus
I gather shells, wet feathers.
Further out, slick with dew
is an empty canoe.

I clamber inside.
No fish on board, no tackle.
Only oars transparent
as air
light as light
as if sky were rowing
a stream of weightless longing.
Come rain!
Come sun!
I am open to the soaring
open to the pouring.

Daughter, I remember
the last time we met.
Your daughter
how she climbed up the slide.
A violinist played
the setting sea bright.
Little warbler
kingfisher, skylark
all your feathers flying.
Memory, oh stricken sight
a flooding *in of starlight.*

Good Things

I am thankful
for the frost on the roof
a window to see the frost on the roof
passing slender cloud

for my son
full-grown
in the next room
sleeping
for his breathing
the food he ate last night
the bundle of dark words
strangler fig words
he tore open

for St. Christopher
the child he bore on his shoulder
staff probing safe passage
across harrowing water
sudden with suck and rock

for the rising sun
for air
shared
as if that could save us.

Day of Mushrooms

A sodden, murky day.
Smells musty, of decay,
an off-white odour with a hint of compost.

How is it when everything's wet
I think of desert: houses half-buried in sand,
creak of wooden doors leached dry;

skeletons listless in corners,
omens of drought spread by wind
like spores;

think of the rain god Chac-mool,
head worn down by blazing grit
to what it was, a boulder, smooth,

only the cracked mouth
gouged deeper, wider, by rude dust—
an empty hollow that still pleads for rain.

Quiet in the quiet
I listen to mushrooms grow
beneath brown leaves.

Dun

Colour of missing
rain, fugitive
in sinkhole, cenote
ear of god
that would hear
the voice of drowning.

Colour of coughing
earth anemic
pyramids of hunger, acacia thorns of thirst
ritual tightened
scuff of your small-bound feet
along a slow lame road.

Colour of pleading
face a blue veil
you beg for rain, song of animal, flower
child you sing for child
cloth pressed
against small breasts.

Colour of piercing
voice
through opaque ear. Drowned
you rise, take wing as eagle
infant scree, scree circling the temple
the earless skull of Chichen Itza.

Collecting Silence

A red-winged blackbird squawks.
Loud. Again. Warning.

At night who knows what the earth has in mind.
We let it disappear into its burrow.

A drop of water before it falls off a leaf.
Collecting silence.

When earth beats its flower drum we follow.
Pollen, pistil, stamen.

We create maps, signs, stories to hold onto.
Yet we are always flying, earth our wingspan.

Ocean Wilderness

Beneath hundred-year-old cedars
a red earth path to the bay,
slope of forty-five degrees as in our Toronto garden
where long ago we tobogganed in deep snow
our leg-over-leg embrace
from you to me and child to child
a memory still stamped on my body as I walk
between wild hedges of salal to glistening ocean
memory a pebble of light that skips over water, sinks
beneath waves off Phang Nga Bay,
water warm as skin, so clear
I could read a book resting on white sand.
All play, I dive with dolphins,
give chase under brilliant sun,
tuck a briny pebble into my pocket, ride
the scrape of incoming tide to Paddle River,
frozen now, Alberta muskeg country.
Slip-slide with family on unaccustomed skates, whack
hockey pucks past the frantic dog into snowbanks.
Until ice groans its thin barrier.
Green hills close in
with their prescription of now,
sea, kin no longer.

I walk back up the narrow path
wet soil stuck to my feet, pluck
a broad leaf round as the world
a stinkbug wobbling at its centre.

– II –

spilling over the wall

blue asters

sky

Walls

It's not a sheltered world.
It's the pressure from the other side of the wall . . .
The walls are a part of you.

     —Tomas Tranströmer, "Vermeer"

   i

It's not a sheltered world.

She builds a mirror-self
stone upon stone
past ankle
calf, thigh
the bay of her waist
promontory of shoulder
up to the keystone.

Leaves a window
for small air
last light

a key song.

Lift the hair from your eyes, her lover asks.
What towers there?

Birds nesting in cracks.

He calls.
Let your hair comb down.
Let the strands fall.
Let your hair weave a desert meadow.
Let us lie in the wild rose of its song.

She calls.

He climbs.
Eyes fragile as eggs.

ii

It's the pressure from the other side of the wall . . .

On the great wall that divides the city
she reads words that look like birds,
wings spread wide.

A train-less night.
Trompe l'oeil windows lit by laughter
flash by.

She longs for red bicycles with silver handles,
golden spokes new and shiny.
They rise up in her dreams and wheel away
down a long avenue on the other side.
Elixir, delicious, green rosette of Rapunzel.
Devil's claw. Rust-eyed.

She leaps.
Breaches longitudes.
Compass in her pocket.
She leaves her hungerchild, hinterchild
in the house of decrepitude.
This unjust balance.

He steals across no-man's land
risks buried mines
bullets lodged in his heels, like wings.
Climbs over an equator of walls
to the other side.
His eyes: a declaration, antelope leap
bean stalk.
His belly, a veined book
full of lust.

Who has the calloused hands?
Who the wrung heart?

iii

The walls are a part of you.

She lives in a house without doors.
Knocks from inside.
Does not know how it grew around her
stone upon stone.
She climbs the ribs of the walls.
All she sees is moss and lichen.
Jumps for joy at the odd spider.
Cannot decipher its tiny language.
She knocks. Knocks until there is a hole into sky.
The colour so strong it walks right through her.

Watchdog

after Alex Colville's painting, Willow

She sits on the edge of the open trunk of their car.
She holds a small jar, insufficient for a journey.
The trunk is almost empty. They cannot have come from far.

A man sits on the ground before her, calm, in no hurry
to rise, go elsewhere. Her other hand, resigned, lies in her lap.
Between her feet a dog, protective, alert. It does not scurry.

There are no birds here. No flicks of chatter to snap
her quiet air as she rests between tail lights, large as pylons.
Signals. Heart's road torn up, blind hole dug deep. To tap

into a new foundation. His back is straight as thought. Eyes on
his wife's bowed head, hair white and smooth, unlike the willow
branches overhead, green cascade, a fountain. Bygones.

A soundless dirge engulfs the car and trunk, dark pillow
of the willow nest. She's closed her eyes. Nothing more to say.
He gazes across the deepening brook of silence, hollow.

The dog stares straight ahead. Still, the weighted day.

The False Mirror

Magritte's painting of an eye
startle of blue sky and white clouds

the eye to all appearance
strenuously blind

to the woman, how
the sun of a thousand questions
burns in the nape of her neck

the man, how
his stories deny exit
chafe like swallowed gravel in her throat

their home
a loss
a hunger faster than now

shell
scraped bare
meat from bone

in each cold breath
splintered glass
paws of silence restive in the walls;

how, wilding
the four-legged roof
tracks back and forth

howls
hackles raised
in the wake of the falling moon.

Magritte, himself silent
goes for a walk—
same time every day

hat on head
little dog by his side
on a leash.

The False Mirror: The title given to Magritte's painting by Belgian
surrealist writer Paul Nougé.

Mona Lisa

who does not know you

iconed
x-rayed on history's gurney, flesh cold
measured
the drop or lift
of left or right upper lip
or lower
cameras on selfie sticks bristle-strut
send portraits home

how small you are

fast in a gilded frame
your eyes
spring snowmelt
running of the bulls in Pamplona
your mouth
a small Syrian child
washed up on Bodrum's shore
face down.

Newcomers

Sun pugnacious.

Stray dogs, teats generations dry.
Shredded plastic bags,
faint smell of dahl and rice,
car exhaust, heat, honking.

We sit in air-conditioned safety
in a restaurant in Mumbai.
I smoothe the linen napkin on my lap.
Day's special, lobster bisque and pasta primavera
fragrance of frangipani.

Sun punches higher.

We chatter, laugh.
Look outside.
See a young man, a sari-clad woman
standing like an abandoned building,
stand and silently stare at us.
See them wait long bells of hours, lean
into each other, sway as one,
faces a ghostwritten plea
hands empty.

Haze of high-noon sun.

My hand slows
as I pass butter for the bread.
Anxiety gnaws at my ankles
with quick sharp teeth—
leap!
through black window
here to there.

Doors open, close.
The man, the woman, still standing.

Who can decipher the words
stranded on the tightrope
of our hidden lives?

Hear heart's paper
tear into masks, beaks
that open, close . . . whisper?

What hunger chooses silence?

Brink Year

ink of newspaper cracks, crumbles into slag heaps
words take on the mystery of spiders in deep burrows

days rust-red
bootless, echoless

winded
hung

I descend into cave, into permafrost, a hiding place
among mammal bones, forgotten history

into a blue crevasse where blue lashes will mark my sleep
and ice will carve me into sculpture, prove I once existed

to emerge one day in the colours of lichen
subsistence food in hard times.

Separation

i

Cows

Sentries behind the electric fence.
The old farmhouse uprooted
from its hole-in-the-ground foundation.

ii

Crosses

Rows of names
straight as bullets to the horizon.
A granite soldier scrapes blue from the sky.

iii

Son

Your father's death
a tinder-dry hole of absence.
Each day, unblinking, you burn.

Intertidal

The moon tells us to look for what might be lost.
It's not a big help. It has no eyes, no ears.

There was a time everyone dressed up for travel.
New jackets, pants. Shoes polished and shined.

Hudson Bay, rain-lashed. Canoes heavy with furs.
In the parking lot of The Bay, cars slick with rain.

I walk behind my daughter. As tall as me now. Quickness
of smolt on their way to open ocean.

The sea comforts even in the dark. Strokes the shore.
Grains of sand glisten. Intertidal. Shushing.

Charcoal Portrait

Portrait of a woman hanging on the wall,
soft charcoal. She is naked. She looks down
and to the side, into a golden wall.

Portrait. Eyes, nose, mouth, hair pulled back, head high.
A woman. Which woman? The one who lost her son? Her lover?
And she, left alone to hang on the wall, hidden behind
soft charcoal, edges darkened, background darker still, stripped
naked, no arms, no hands to hold. Nipples soft as eyes
that look down and to the side
into a bare golden wall.

The Fourth Monk

In this feng shui house of open doors and windows
three golden monks as tall as my hand
perch on a bedroom bookshelf
direct the winds of good fortune.
A fourth hangs from a pipe beneath the kitchen sink,
glints in the dark.

Today is good-fortune day. Two graduations.
Our daughter, grade twelve, in a dress as tight as her curves,
impatient with my hands as I comb her hair,
rushes past the raised teak threshold to expectant friends.
Our son, shoulders a finger's breadth above mine,
soon to enter grade nine, refuses to attend.
The ceremony for him a three-legged waltz.
An hour to go, he changes his mind.
My alarm bells rampage. Whirlwind dress-up begins.

A hermit crab trying a new shell, he slips into my husband's suit.
Jacket down to the knees, white shirt untucked.
Pant waist below buttocks. So cool, he insists.
But I buckle it high, waist so tiny my hands almost span it.
Pant legs still five inches too long. Everything droops,
like ice cream melting over a cone,
puddling.

A lesson in tying a tie, the easy-over and under.
I pull up his collar, pause. My hand brushes soft neck hairs
unshaven, moist, warm, a surreptitious caress. I miss it already.
He tries on black shoes. Shuffles, loses them.
My heart aches for the small gap he will fill too soon,
the small step that will open the moon.
A short while later he walks out the door
pant legs stuffed into the backs of white sneakers, laces untied.

Silence.
Outside a green snake
winds its way up the brown trunk of a palm tree,
emerald flash in sunlight—
and vanishes into the leaves.

Edmonton's Royal Jubilee Auditorium

Cold crunches with clenched teeth tonight.
It does not let go. My hands are red and stiff.

A heavy coat weighs me down. Slip it off.
I long to be newly clothed.

Up that flight of steps. Two at a time. Plush red carpet.
My feet know more than I do.

There's a campfire here. Under a starry sky.
Amulets of song and story to adorn me.

Curtains open. The stage is empty. Then takes from me
what I most desire. I watch and listen. Become kindling.

My Day's Full Beauty

Orange spark on the tip of a tall spruce.
A hummingbird.
I blink, and it's gone.

I close my eyes. See it again.
Like sunlight striking a dead leaf,
and it silvers.

Late in the long hot day
drizzle draws the shades.
In the half-light of then and now

my mother darns socks.
We sit side by side on a sofa
listening to Monteverdi's *Orfeo*.

Hear love and longing break. Summer
spark of a Christmas tree ornament.
Gleam on a remote mountain.

Curriculum Vitae

I live between pebbles in the moist dark. Sprout. Sleep
like a ladder leaning against a cloud. A camel, cat, a mouse.

Get up in the morning, stuff yesterday into my back pocket
next to chewed gum.

I permit thought. Like oatmeal, I try to eat it every morning.
It is good for me. Makes me glow like a desert on fire.

I float my broken things down a river in a canoe
made of salted wounds.

Weave myself into a basket made of wax. Gather
the honey of the world.

Three Wishes

Today the dandelion's head is a platter of gold.
Tomorrow, seed-ball, white lisp of wind.

Time is a small animal beside my bed, nose moist,
snuffling. I wake up to feed it.

Does water know when it is tea?
Does the watermelon know when it is cut?

When trees are still and there is only sky
I am heartbeat, chambered rosary of time.

The books I read as a child are still the same.
The three wishes I once held are now red apples.

Tide

One day
I noticed
the bones in my hands
raised like ridges of sand
left by a receding tide.
I thought of caves
hollowed by water and time,
walls glowing golden
with all that has vanished,
small statues of gods.

Visit to South Haven Cemetery

Sky, a four-lane highway in rush-hour traffic.
Past the edge of town
city clatter—air graffiti—fades.
Dust lisps along the floorboards
of abandoned houses, rusted cars.

We enter the long field of silence.
Headstones regular as a prairie fence
that catches winter snow.
Walls for urns. Locked doors.
All is sheared.
Easy-access lawn, wayward flowers.

Another friend gone, you say
petals pulled on a daisy.

Beside a snowmobile wreck
an empty bench, nothing to weigh it down.
Embedded in scarred metal
the framed photo of a young man.
The glass reflects sky, fleeting clouds.
A magpie pecks at the shiny frame, hops away.
In his high school yearbook friends will have written:
Great guy. Most likely to succeed—
and, *Love you. Always.*

Nearby, on granite
a man's name, date of death
the space beside his name still vacant.
On his grave, plastic flowers
wind-angled bandage
brittle.

There's a bin for weeds, a bin for water.
You dig the narrow strip of garden
that hugs the family stone
prairie soil a dry, hard scab. Plant flowers
to anchor sun's yellow.

Time fattens, thins.
The spruce grows another inch taller.
Tarnish deepens, names fill in.
Sorrows slip underside
become tiny word poems
bless
protect
like black seeds beneath fronds of ferns.

Hazard Note

The door opens.
Poetry slips in
wraps itself around my throat
digs in with claws of contentment
kneading.

My voice strums the hazard note
grapples with breath
backs into the forest
to limber, stretch, arch,
learn to see in the dark.

I've always known
something struggles in the woods
torch of swamp cabbage
watery roots
a rough tongue.

Conversation

In memory of my grandmother Frieda Schultz,
b. Conradi (1901–2002), a Baltic-German deeply
rooted in her homeland Latvia, her life shaped by
the Russo-Japanese war (1905), the Bolshevik
Revolution, WWI, a great depression, forced
emigration (1939), WWII, and finally, emigration
to a peaceful new home in Canada (1952).

I could not discern the moment you left.

You were just no longer,
a snowflake melting
it seemed so easy.

I could not discern—
until a coldness rolled in
a morning mist
sinking warmth beneath it
until it drowned.

My hand on your neck
then on my heart,
a slow goodbye our only conversation now
of the many we once had
between beers
and irregular Russian verbs,
foreign words that were survival fare
for you on the front.
Learn the language of your enemies
you always said.
But I, I loved its sound.

Your life spanned a century of shovel and spade.
You dug the soil of altered tectonics,
of two world wars,
and a revolution you'd quickly add
of which you remembered only
fire,
which when it died sank deep
into the peat of your days
smouldered subterranean while you watered
the flowers by your window.

Our last time together
we leaned
each into the other
bypassed all else
read a children's story
we both had known well
of a child with a basket
eating berries
in a big-berried blueberry forest.

Trestle Bridge Nightmare

night circles night
slips through the well-dark hole of my eye
wings shiver

double-dared
I straddle hungry rails
above a cactus canyon
dream faces without names   no partner
to steady me here   abandoned
by the guide—
that thief

fear snows in

moon
mumbles
muddles direction, ties me in knots

where is the safety of the other side?

I stumble
fall

into dream
gold-flecked, triumphant
        each note
                a step
                        my body can walk on.

Crater Lake

We walk towards the lip of the crater
along a well-worn path. Far below us, the lake.
God's protean eye lined with kohl refracts the sky.

Amazing that no water has ever drained from this caldera.
Prehistoric lizards and other unimaginable creatures
have scrambled down its slippery slopes to drink.
Some slid in, perished.

A wooden boat ramp floats
on water the colour of charred pine.
Not even the delicate hairs on the feet of water striders
mar its unblemished surface.
Light glints. Wind sends a shiver.

I sit on the ramp, dip my toes in,
hesitant, as if I need permission,
think back to summers in the Okanagan
and submerging in water warm as ripe melon.

Here we could have swum as Adam and Eve,
the lake an offering all to ourselves. Diving in,
knocked on the door of creation.

But we do not enter. The lake's measure too deep.
So deep and black a stone's fall,
a body's fall, would seem endless.
We sense a serpent waiting,
cold eye patient.

– III –

seaweed

rocking on slow waves

a passing ferry

Ghost Lilies

Michigan Central Station. Tall ruin, ashen on rainy days.
Inside, an opera singer reverses the emptying tide.
Voice strong and clear—a spring shower,
shimmering lake, flamingo swarm.
Pilgrim, entranced, I watch long necks, legs, wings
burst forth from beaux-arts windows.
Air quivers pink.

Underpass in old Riga. Steady tramp of footsteps.
The thrumming rushes me
past a mother, young son, rooted, leafless
as trees submerged by waters of a dam.
Violin and voice. Cap on ground. For prayer, a lullaby:
"May you grow strong, little bear, *aijā žūžū,*
honey and berries, hush-a-bye."
Shine, little boy, like the fish
that still flash for me on fragrant days
in the silver tarn of your song.

Strasbourg cathedral. Slender saints, gothic spires.
My eyes drawn high. Until stone gives way
to a riderless sound— arrow pulled tight.
Bowing the horsehead fiddle, *morin khuur,*
four young Mongolian men
seated in the vast and crowded square
throat-sing wind-scoured longing. Transported,
I, with them, legs taut, race bareback over rolling plain,
breathe in sweet scent of taiga grass in spring.
Shaking the snow globe of that time
I'm tuned again
as sound flakes swirl around apostles,
tourists drinking coffee in cafes, laughter on a sunny day.

Cathedral of St. Eustache in Paris. Sombre hulk.
I wander deep inside the stone-arced dark.
Hear small white-flower voices lap and babble, shoreless.
An African woman in blue and white habit
kneels, head lowered, in dialogue, it seems,
with something in the distance, homegrown, ocean-strewn.
She looks at me. Her glance a net; eyes, crocus bloom.

Outside, two stone sculptures by Henri de Miller.
One, a giant egg-shaped hairless head tilted sharply sideways.
One, a giant hand cupped by the ear.
Écoute, the title. *Listen.*
A girl climbs from fingertip to nose tip. A boy sits
on the open eye.

Ghost Lilies: The name the people of Detroit use for lilies that continue
coming up in gardens of abandoned houses.

Hollows

Snow blows in broad swathes on the prairie, fills every hollow.

It must have looked the same the winter you were captured
on the Russian steppe.

You never said much about it.

Only how the snow kept falling
and the border kept shifting
until the troops left you behind.
A young doctor, you stayed
with the wounded.

To hide, to harbour the sick
you slipped into a ditch
slid wedding ring into your shoe
huddled, watching crystals of snow trickle
down from the ridge filling footprints, the fear,
like a rabbit in its burrow sensing a ferret near.

Once released, you returned.

It's Christmas Eve.
You knock on the door of a house
still standing. Step inside.
My sister sees you, jumps into your arms
cries "Papi, Papi."
My mother stands speechless, unmoving.
She does not recognize your body
your eyes.

Snow blows and blows.

Patch of Land, Liepāja, Latvia

We peer through a rusting fence. A large neglected field,
the graves of Jews, earth shuffling bones like cards.

Roma tend their small plots. They turn away from us,
hats low, looks askance.

A tall cross silhouetted against the setting sun.
Its shadow lengthens over fallen soldiers, Latvian,

Russian, German. We seek a relative, long gone,
his tombstone lost in overgrown forest.

He was a doctor who sheltered his brother
and bride for a night as they fled for their lives.

Memories fade. Cities bulldoze tombstones,
make cemeteries into parks where children play.

Clear-cut

A rush of longing, that soft worn chair.

I want to go home, she says
her house sold long ago.

Memory clear-cut
a white flag of surrender to sleep on.

When she stumbles
there's no sweet moss to catch her.

Each step a new Columbus
terra incognita of faces once held close.

Paths do not lead to shelter.

Indiscriminate target
the mind.

Violence Seems Unreal for a While

after Tomas Tranströmer, "Out in the Open"

i

a deer breathes
a white cloud
cedars in snow

Damascus invades my West Coast room.
On TV, war. Smoke billowing in the emptied spaces
of bombed-out houses.
Rubble. Voiceless streets.

I see you, little daughter, on a hospital bed,
legs blown off.
See in your eyes what you see,
the ghost of loss—
of the walk to school,
to buy bread in the market,
of shoes and socks.
A stone too heavy to carry.

Sweet round-faced girl, your scarf carefully tied.

The ghost voracious, eats and eats.
I, too, now stunned by loss.

ii

   spring rain
   new grass bends
   with the rushing stream

Little girl, you float on a leaf, fly, a bird
but the dark fur of earth awaits.

You light a candle on night's leaf,
earth's red wine awaits.

A bird still and cold lies at your feet,
you wrap warm breath around her—
earth's blind mole awaits.

You burn, I burn, a candle bright
in night's dark grief.

iii

   blackberries
   warm and ripe
   our purple hands

Summer storm.
The sun explodes, is levelled by clouds
explodes again, is slashed by trees.
Wind washes rain through the cuts.
By evening, blistering strips bandage the horizon.
We can come out now
in our dusk-red skirts of mourning.

When Sky Leaps

blue
is spring seed
mouth's hunger

My mother puts blue placemats on the table
a basket of bread in the centre
moves the vase with flowers to the sideboard

blue
is morning glory
Himalayan poppy

She prunes the Christmas cactus, too big now for the pot
sweeps away dead petals
a few flowers still in bloom

blue
thick with all the world
is pulse, sweet fontanel

She buys cake and a newspaper
for old friends in the hospital
his wife unable to talk, he to walk

oh, to pull down ribbons of blue
tie them to ankle and wrist
make us stride with long strides

She gives me a watch, passed from mother
to mother, gold face, gold hands
it always loses time

Peaks

Is God the wind? my son asked.

—Genevieve Lehr, "The latter half of the
 third quarter of the waning moon"

i

Ararat. Standard-bearer of faith.
Peak rises bright above the receding flood,
world left bare beneath.
Hunger seeds in waterlogged earth.
How can I follow the dove?

ii

Holy Mount Kailash.
Pilgrims circumnavigate the base
on hands, knees, bellies,
inch forward grey with worship,
eyes to the ground.
Trucks rumble by, spitting gravel.

iii

On the dry, rocky road up Mount Sinai
only burning bush and stone tablets
strict with commandments, badges of hope
borne on the back of exile.
Not even a glimmer of water.

iv

Mount Olympus.
Once solid.
Gods now storyboard, puzzles
spun by Aeolian winds in faint dreams.
To vanish by dawn, rose keening.

v

Everest. Highest. Most human.
Littered with efforts at apotheosis,
the need to drape ourselves in mountain,
in stuttering wind that makes the ice
in our veins, fire.
Pockmarked with shrill glittering remnants
of longing.

vi

On top of Alaska's Mount Denali, awestruck,
I stand within a cone of wind,
a moaning tone, last call.
Is God the wind?
I turn, and turn, find only myself.
My shouts leave barely a track
on the long steep slope of white.

vii

Uluru, Ayers Rock.
Sun-filled belly of earth, wide and flat.
Ochre crayon pressed thick layer upon layer.
Carving down, I find . . . ancient coral worlds.
I read their shell-starred palm,
a language
sacred.

In the Beginning

Woman

was wordless

Fire stoked

the embers beneath her ribs

She became song

strung on a desert harp

Song became spirit

antelope with lion's mane

springbok

No wonder she dances

so fleet and light

Darkness but a contrabass.

Blue and White Pottery

Qing dynasty shards dredged from the Chao Phraya River.
We glue them back together. Make new patterns.

16th-century Goa. A woman bites off a toe of the incorruptible
body of St. Francis Xavier. To test if it's real.

Today I walk on felt feet, leave the world to other conductors.
Pen in hand, I sit in the honey of morning. Wait for bees.

The robin, its body a-burst with chirps, beak marking beats,
tail flicking. I'm envious. If only it wouldn't eat all my cherries.

I once sat in Chopin's garden, listening to his music.
My ears grew big, luxurious, moss-green. Transplantable.

After the Opera on Humboldt Street

The doors open.
Mozart's *Così fan Tutte* just finished.
We collect our coats, walk up the aisle,
talk of the beautiful voices,
how the maid was the best,
walk slowly behind the lady with the cane
and all the others, average age, oh, sixty-five,
our brochures now old, some left behind.
There's talk of love, the impossibility
of fidelity,
but not for long,
each of us carries our own song
into the foyer where we crowd round,
inch forward, step outside.
Stop, surprised,
the night thick with pink blossoms
that tumble around us in lamp-lit arcs,
brush our uplifted faces
with a blush, as if with rapture.

Petals gather in wide bands by the roadside,
silk ribbons.
How lucky we are to see what will be gone tomorrow
swept away by the wind.
Even now a breeze stirs the petals
as we leave, step from sidewalk to street
tiptoe through this fragile fringe,
something we wish to keep—
a riffle of love and spring
whispering
whispering

Oh *mia bella.*

– IV –

an eagle

circling the sun . . .

field of daisies

Somewhere a Ferry

Suddenly, something approaches the window.
I stop working and look up.
The colours blaze. Everything turns around.
The earth and I spring at each other.

— Tomas Tranströmer, "Face to Face"

It is an ordinary day here.
Somewhere a ferry
capsizes, sinks.
Obeying orders, 300 children
wait, curled up like hedgehogs
under tables and chairs, winnow
fear. Mother, where are you?
Father, can you hear? Darkness
lowers its visor, draws its bow.
Suddenly, something approaches the window.

It is an ordinary day here.
Somewhere fires
leap fences, crash doors,
eat all the breakfasts,
plunder beds.
What to salvage? What give up?
Everyone fleeing.
Something's forgotten,
mewling and curled up.
I stop working and look up.

It is an ordinary day here.
Somewhere an ice shelf
cracks and floats far out to sea.
The rising chill.
Something's stranded, pacing, black.
Light falling. That sound.
Elsewhere children play soccer.
Lawn mowers carve their usual patterns.
Summer windborne, outward-bound.
The colours blaze. Everything turns around.

An ordinary day.
Somewhere a ferry.
I stop working and look up.
Sprays of blue
wisteria, sky entwine.
Silken lovers.
My darkened eye
ash-flecked
grief with no cover.
The earth and I spring at each other.

Frolic

When I step outside and the air is cool,
I don't know whether to shiver or laugh.

Birds take their frolic into the trees. They are almost full,
boughs bouncing. How lucky.

Grass hides many things—moss, violets, buttercups.
When mown, everything's pale.

The arbutus trees have a fungus. Cold makes it worse.
How do they bear their black wounds, leaves brown and curled?

I pick up a stone and throw it as far as I can. It turns bird,
many birds with bright wings. I ride their song.

Anniversary

Like clothes on a line saying
"You will live long enough to wear me."

—Naomi Shihab Nye,
"Arabic Coffee"

We vowed: One day
you will know me well enough to wear me.

Fox fur, beaver pelt, a little dry and brittle
stacked or hanging.
Still the silver wind, underwater den of winter
prairie beyond the fort, grey-green smell of sagebrush.

The way your hand reaches for where my step
flows into yours, for where I fall back to catch up.

I repeat lines and say I want you with me in these lines.

Your light-blue polyester suit, "pearly everlasting" blossoms
crumbled in a pocket.
My leather miniskirt, packed, unpacked.
Your glasses black, then silver-framed, then frameless.
I too begin to wear glasses, see
the years soften like cashmere.

A squirrel
grey as a weathered fence
tail, flicks of butternut gold
grasps in its paws a dried corn cob
rushes off.

You said last night:
It's going to rain. I'll take the pillows in.

This morning, sky
cerulean, drenched naked
wears our forty-year-old promise.

Eclipse

The moon
a mottled yolk now rich with glowing reds
lifts from its pasted background
hovers
     suspended
         almost close

roundness
fit to pluck and hold

    like love

close enough to take a bite out of.

David Bowie on the Malahat

Windshield wipers swish back and forth. Highway
in and out of focus, slick with a layer of wet ice.
Lights glisten. We drive past Goldstream Park
where salmon come to spawn and die. Feast for eagle, bear.
Douglas fir and cedar, black with a sprinkle of white.
Snow thickens, closes in. Bays, hills of the Malahat gone.
Our little capsule warm and bright. Skis in back.
Radio reports—snow on Mt. Washington, high.

Chris Hadfield interrupts our cottony thoughts.
He's singing "Space Oddity," David Bowie's
odyssey song. We catch *tin can, ground control,*
countdown, detach from station, hum with him,
wing, float with him weightless, strumming a guitar—
all of us, Earth, music—a slim lens of light
sparkling in *a most peculiar way* in deep night.

Forward to Mars

Up high where the water tower squats
and wisps of grey lichen hang
from scrub trees

we sit cross-legged, picnic
on wine, olives, hummus, crackers
in this sunny spot where the wind is private.

Look out over trees, the Strait of Georgia, islands
into blue sky fading to black, inky magnet
you, Friedel, scanned

telescope in hand, through a hatch in the roof
a boy drawn to Mars
by the lure, in space, of life.

A man, ill, starving, in a freezing lab far from home
you pulled ideas and numbers together
designed GIRD-X
          snow was surely falling in Moscow

the first liquid-fuelled rocket
to blast toward space . . .
a few months after you died.

In a photo, edges worn
you, coat too large, gaze out at us
eyes fevered.

Lit fuse of awe, eyes echoing yours
we stowaway on the spacecraft
New Horizons

hurtle past Pluto into greater black
old beyond thought,
discover there

just a whisper of matter, strange
invisible matter, vertigo
dark, ever darker.

We take a deep breath, slow down
touch stone, shiver
wrapped in cool spring sun

hear in age-old dry-grass quiet
seed coats open
light sprigs crown from dark.

Forward to Mars: The motto of my great-uncle Friedrich Zander (1887–1933),
a Baltic-German pioneer of rocketry and space flight in the Russian Empire
and the Soviet Union. From my father, Gerhard Conradi, I learned that
Friedel, the familiar name of Friedrich, had named his daughter Astra, his
son Merkur.

Harijan

Her hands spread mud on the walls of her house
make it new after each rain—hands soft and brown as mud.

The old woman, voice strong as a zebu,
sari shielding her face from the cameraman, says:
I am nothing. You are god.
Do something.

> *I am mud*
> *stacked stones*
> *a house dried by sun*
> *circle of thatched roof.*

> *In the shade of my house children are music*
> *mud of my walls*
> *stones*
> *twirling sun*
> *a royal court.*

> *I am kalbelia gypsy, dancer, untouchable*
> *my house is landless*
> *mud, stones*
> *cracked sun.*
> *We once enchanted kings.*

> *I am nothing*
> *stones of my house*
> *now stacked*
> *beside the new road.*

The cameraman films
one hour
his eyes etched
road
beginning and end
untouchable
god.

Harijan: Mahatma Gandhi popularized this term as applied to the formerly
untouchable caste, the Dalit. It means "child of God."

Mountains of Meteora

Thick thumbs poke the dough of heaven.
Monasteries, like cockscombs, balance on top.
At the base of narrow rock-hewn steps, scrawny dogs.
Tourists throng like lemmings. All this heat. Inside a church,
hell dips a finger in the marrow of sickled souls. Ignites walls.
Gold flecks dust down on monks, two young, three old.
We are clappers inside this golden bell, striking.

Nearby another black-rimmed icon. Our group squeezes in.
We breathe the ancient yeasty breath of martyred saints,
become owls. See, huddled in corners, refugees,
the locked caskets of their hearts.

In the garden a young nun squats to tend flowers.
A silver cross dangles at her breast, a tiny clock, a playful swing.
Late afternoon mist rises like prayer
past violets up the mountain.
We lose all bearings, remember only violets.
They blink like stars.
Birds flit in and out, in and out.

Night. More powerful than night, a sound,
rolls of thunder urgent in our sleep.
How the mountains shift, and scour,
as though drowning.

Lament

Masks hang on the wall
of the longhouse

in Alert Bay, Cormorant Island
one in particular

wooden head, hollow, no eyes
lips round and pursed as a tornado

Dzunukwa
someone knew her

carved
Dzunu hu huu huu kwa!

giant wild woman stalker
black-fanged cry

how she hunted on the run
frightened children in dark woods

huddles now among fern headstones
soughs among tall trees, bark fissured, chapped

caws a last song
breathes in the last sap

as surly winds rake up a cover
feathers black ravens

her mouth, protruding
a blind worm blowing a long lament.

Extinction

Gabriel . . . was the angel
who had to hold his breath because
his trumpet could spell the end of things.

—Lorna Crozier,
        "Tobias's Dog and the Angel"

i

Black egg of our heart, stillborn.

Once, like locusts
passenger pigeons haloed the sky
a flock
300 miles long, one mile wide
took 14 hours to pass by

as if this could never be lost . . .

1914, in the Cincinnati Zoo
Martha, last of her kind,
died

left behind
wingprints in air

the iris radials of our eyes
all bone and feather.

ii

Amelia Earhart
listens
the drone of her plane falters

the Pacific below

face, hands enter quiet
stone angel at her side
wings folded.

iii

Hildegard von Bingen
Listen: there was once a king . . .
it pleased the king to raise a small feather
from the ground
and he commanded it to fly. The feather flew,
not because of anything in itself but because
the air bore it along.
Thus am I
a feather on the breath of God.

iv

Genghis Khan, stone warrior
strokes the soft sunlit back of his pigeon
sends it
red eyes, red legs
homing
a bloodline of war.

v

We walk miles of dark
time
beneath black rain, burning planes
bland mud choked on letters home
sky-torn.

vi

Still among us
carrier pigeon, wild rock pigeon
war pigeon
50 miles per hour for 1,000 miles
secret messenger
slipstream of hope
unerring, true.

One alone vanished
veered unseen
to her mate, a nest
blue sky in her egg

wild homing.

Rim Light

As the world grows bigger
you and I grow smaller.

Outside the window a woodpecker kowtows
his way up a tall dead pine,
fat grubs a reward.

We lie on our bed
curled around the womb of our years.

Dust balls skitter beneath,
loose ends
sadness, glory.

Sun slips to the other side.
Last rays trace our outline.
Luster.

A woodpecker kowtows
his way up a tall dead pine.

Birds perch on bare branches.
Notes on a staff.
Melody. Sky.

Grand Staff of Music

In the beginning was the Word

Scra-a-a-ck, crust breaks
turtle peers out
on its back the voices of all peoples
a rollicking, clambering crescendo
of sound, octaves of words

With this music we built

The library at Nineveh
stacks of cuneiform, word-lyre fired in clay
King Ashurbanipal could read, he said
inscriptions from before the Flood
look into the future
divine the will of the gods

A new scale

Alphabet cathedral
rose-window light
pipe organ spilling letters
illuminated manuscripts
sound poems

We sit in a field of pews, inhale
exhale in the key of grace
remote lives coming ever closer
baton, fish-tail snap
kingfisher's feather—luminous
blue-green prism split
into bell clang

Glory

Testing Balance

Sparrows on a wire huddle together.
Test balance. Make room for one more.

A plane carries passengers like eggs in a carton.
Free-range; thin shells hold.

The woman pushes a shopping cart along Beacon Avenue.
She wears her grey hood so low there's no room for hello.

A dog curls against a man sleeping on the street.
In front a bright red tomato. Like an eye. Awake.

Long prairie grass bends with the wind towards earth.
We are grass, ears tuned to the ground.

Blinding White

Spring cleaning. I follow the objects of my life.
Who's tailing who?

A photo of my son and me beside a big old tiger.
We are far from home. Maybe the tiger has forgotten.

A man dressed in blinding white sits beside a train track
on a garbage-strewn street in Mumbai. He smiles. What a smile.

A boy begs for money to buy polish for his shoeshine business.
The Oberoi's marble steps already polished.

Rhododendrons bloom. My basket overflows:
gulmohar flowers, bougainvillea, lotus, marigolds, orchids.

An Offering

The sarus crane, 1.5 metres tall! high-steps his way
to a mate. In his beak an offering of straw. Spring. Dungarpur.

A basket woven of cedar bark. How simple it looks.
It isn't. It holds secrets. Cedar secrets.

Spiders are master weavers. So are some ants.
But that's nothing. They learned it all from the wind.

How do I know this? I ask you: who can weave a web—
invisible threads so strong they hold the world.

I learned a new language when you were born.
It is one we all know without speaking.

White Postcards

after Tomas Tranströmer, "Black Postcards"

i

The calendar pages blank, the days chaos.
But birds sing, each song a country. Passport
in my pocket. Sunshine blankets the sea, hides
               armadas of storms.

ii

Not long ago I touched death. It reached
through my fingers to my bones. We held hands
for a while. Life goes on. But something is tracking
               my heartbeat, counting.

Femme Assise

after the portrait of Jaime Sabartés,
Le bock, *by Pablo Picasso, 1902*

Rain stirs the blues.
Straight-backed, gaze lowered, the woman
sits out the silky swirl and glimmer of the dance.
Abandoned. Yet again.
Lips thinned.
Eyes shadowed,
to blunt boom and scratch of memory.
Lost now
her faith that goodness rises like oil on water
as birthright, birthmark,
a peony of blood embedded in skin—
when pressed it flushes deeper.
Where solace?

Night lists towards morning, rolls rain into gutters.
Come sun
she touches her face, blue wash of rain,
turns her hands into linden-scented wind
to bring back waltz and tango;
lights midsummer's pyre, flames
devouring the gnash of loss;
stretches high on her toes
becomes the smoke of its burning
a crackling greenwood song ascending
in clear calm air . . . a signal

not unlike the call of wolves
the call of whales
on long stretches between rain-drenched seas.

Pietà

by Michelangelo

Grief has grown large in her lap.

Flow of sorrow, white, marble
cold to the touch
how it lines the curve of her belly.

Eyes carved closed
his
and hers
Mary unable to let go what has already fallen
let go
the shoulder sliding
the unbearable weight.

In the basilica
rain.

Her open palm.

ABOUT THE AUTHOR

Ulrike (Conradi) Narwani, of Baltic-German heritage, grew up in Edmonton. She completed a PhD in Slavic Languages and Literatures at the University of Toronto in 1977. Her husband's work shifted the family to the United States, England, India and Thailand, with a final move in 2003 to Sidney, B.C.—moves that provided unexpected and unique opportunities to fulfill their passion for flying. She and her husband have co-written the memoir *Above the Beaten Path*, detailing their adventures flying a single-engine Cessna 182 into remote corners, virtually around the world. Now, nurtured by a vibrant community of local poets, she finds that poetry has become a major part of her life. Her work has appeared in *Island Writer*, *CV2*, two chapbooks, *In That Wild Place* and *Vanishing into the Leaves* (edited by Patrick Lane) and the anthology *Poems from Planet Earth* (edited by Yvonne Blomer and Cynthia Woodman Kerkham). Her poetry placed first in two contests: *Island Writer* (2011) and *FreeFall* (2012); was shortlisted in *Arc* (2009); and received honourable mention in *Vallum* (2013). She and her nephew, Jens Gerbitz, have published a photo/poetry book, *All that You Can't Bear to Lose*. Her haiku have appeared in *Haiku Canada Members' Anthology* (2015, 2016). *Collecting Silence* is her debut volume of poetry. She makes her home in North Saanich, B.C.